CUCKOO FOR

CUCKOO FOR
KOKOPELLI

BY DAVE WALKER

NORTHLAND PUBLISHING

For their help, interviews, and the generous loan of artwork and merchandise, the publisher wishes to thank the contributors, especially the following: Native Spirit, Sedona; Zonies Galleria, Sedona; Qué Pasa, Phoenix and Scottsdale; Richard Forrest and New West Galleries, Sedona; Steve Pevarnik of Flagstaff; Loona Otero of Parks, Howard Sice of Tucson, Catherine Coughlin at *Arizona Highways*, Robert Shields Design, and Pelli-People, Inc. Thanks also to Jim Geisler of Kokopelli Records for the wonderful CDs, and to Allen Pile of Kactus Jock, Scottsdale, for Dave Walker's favorite new hat.

www.northlandbooks.com

COVER AND PAGE III: *Kokopelli,* air-brushed metal, by Richard Forrest.
Courtesy of New West Galleries
PAGE II: Anasazi pictographs at Kokopelli Cave, Canyon de Chelly National Monument, Arizona
PAGE V: East Kokopelli Street in East Flagstaff, Arizona.
PAGE VI: *Kokopelli Serenade,* gouache with 23-karat gold foil on handmade paper,
by David Dawangyumptewa.
BACK COVER: Jammin' under the Kokopelli dome; Hopi basket by Eleanor Rock,
courtesy of Twin Rocks and Blue Mountain Trading Posts; *Kokopelli,* hand-forged
steel with patina, by Dutch Walker, courtesy of New West galleries.

Photographs by Klaus Kranz unless otherwise indicated as follows:
Jerry Jacka: pages ii, xii, 1, 3 (both), 7, 10, back cover (basket)
Paula Jansen: page 23 (Kokopelli Inn)
Larry Lindahl: page 11
Burly Fish Tattoo: Page 19 (tattoo)
Peter Bloomer; vi
Northland staff: pages iii, v, 14, 40, 44

Composed in the United States of America
Printed in China

ISBN 10:0-87358-732-4
ISBN 13: 978-0-87358-732-7

Library of Congress Cataloging-in-Publication Data

Walker, Dave, date.
Cuckoo for Kokopelli / by Dave Walker.
p.   cm.
Includes bibliographical references and index.
ISBN 0-87358-732-4
1. Kokopelli (Pueblo deity)—Miscellanea.   I. Title.
E99.P9W25 1998
299'.73—dc21   98-8161

683/7.5M/7-98

For my family.
—D.W.

CONTENTS

Prologue *ix*

Chapter One: Kokopelli 101 *1*

Chapter Two: Advanced Kokopelli *15*

Chapter Three: Cuckoo for Kokopelli *25*

Chapter Four: Interview with a Kokopelli *37*

Epilogue *45*

Selected Bibliography *46*

Appendix: Buyer's Guide *47*

Index *50*

Cuckoo for cookies.

PROLOGUE

My introduction to Kokopelli came at a Phoenix-area golf
course named for him. Kokopelli was good to me that day. I
played well. Still, I had no idea who he was. Some kind of
nutty Indian dude, dancing and honking a horn. You go, Koko!

*Note: thumb
through both
edges back to
front and watch
Koko dance.*

ix

Several months later, Kokopelli came to me again, in
the mail. It was a typical delivery, on a typical day. Mr.
Postman brought me bills, hard-to-resist credit-card offers,
and a colorful flier advertising several local businesses.
Flipping through the ads for Chinese-food delivery joints,
carpet-cleaners, and quickie oil-change stations, there he
was. Back bent, dreadlocks tossed skyward—that
flute-tootin' icon was rocking the kiva!

The thing was, the ad—for a kitchen-cabinet company,
as I recall—had no apparent tie to the Southwest, Native
Americans, music, dancing, celebration. It was, after all, a
come-on for dish-storage units. Yet, there he danced.

A few days later, I was waiting at a stoplight
when I spotted him again, this time outlined in
holes poked through a light-fixture sconce on the
wall of a luxury home in central Phoenix.

This string of seeming Koko-coincidences
launched me into a mellow, reflective state,
from which I was drawn by the sound of a horn.
"It's Kokopelli," I thought. "I can hear him. He's
playing for me."

As it turned out, it was not Kokopelli playing
for me, but rather a fellow motorist. The light had
turned green. On I went.

Several weeks later, Kokopelli came to me again. In a
mall, when I wandered, quite by accident, into an
Arizona-themed souvenir shop. There, Kokopelli danced on

Time to make rain!

Glow-kopelli.

x

ball caps and tee shirts, shot glasses and coffee mugs. He blew chorus after tuneful chorus across placemats and napkins, aprons and beverage coasters. This store had golf balls stamped with Kokopelli. Keychains. A night light. An oven mitt.

Kokopelli's image outnumbered the previous knickknack leader—the howling coyote—ten to one. The gila monster and ubiquitous saguaro cactus were well-represented also, but the trinket winds had clearly shifted.

Kokopelli was king.

Until another Southwestern image comes along to knock him off—and that's inevitable, given the tourism industry's ability to turn inventory—Kokopelli will be the region's goodwill ambassador to the world.

Cool, I thought. We could do worse, I guessed. But it was just a guess. I really had no idea who Kokopelli was or what he meant to the original locals. To me and whoever else encountered him in the context of gift shops and golf courses and restaurant menus, Kokopelli seemed like kind of a jestor—a madcap dancing social director. Join the fun, he seemed to say, let's party. Or something.

Fore-pelli.

Zippo-pelli.

Standing there, examining a Kokopelli cigarette lighter, and wondering, "Who was Kokopelli, and what's he doing on boxer shorts at the mall?", I heard his voice.

"Putz!" he said, in the gruff tones of a male in late middle age. "Go easy on the merchandise!"

I looked around. The only other person in the store was the clerk, a young woman deeply involved in a telephone conversation about the soap opera *Days of Our Lives.*

Turning back to the rack of Koko-product, I heard him again.

"You break it, you buy it, bub!" he said. "*Buy* being the operative concept. This ain't a museum, you know."

"Kokopelli," I said, as quietly as possible. "Is that you?"

Silence. The clerk was looking at me now, though her soap opera seminar continued.

Casually, calmly, coolly, I walked out of the store.

An investigation had been opened. My journey into Kokopelli—part vision-quest, part undergraduate term paper, part shopping spree—would take me many places, including the library, the Internet, and long distance directory assistance.

On that day, in that store, I became a Koko-pilgrim.

A welcome mat for the contemporary kiva.

Flute player petroglyph in Monument Valley, Arizona and Utah.

CHAPTER ONE

KOKOPELLI 101

So, my research began. At risk of committing drive-by anthropology, I will now report my only concrete conclusion: Any quest into the ancient heart of Kokopelli will result in as much confusion as enlightenment. There's not a lot of agreement about who he was, or what he means today.

1

To various observers, he was a trader, a trickster, a fertility figure—even an insect. Perhaps Kokopelli was based on a real person or persons. To some of his biggest fans, he's a living spirit of nature, an intermediary between man and heaven.

He can be, at different times, ribald, nurturing, and entertaining. More than anything, I suspect he will remain mostly confounding. Which is, no doubt, one of the more appealing elements of his character. Kokopelli is a multi-purpose mystery man, a something-to- everyone icon who will forever dance across the mesas of our imagination.

Navajo basket by Eleanor Rock. Courtesy of Twin Rocks and Blue Mountain Trading Posts

There are just a few things we "know" about Kokopelli. The rest is educated guesswork and brave extrapolation. Of course, even the stuff we "know" is open to question, contradiction, and reinterpretation. Such is the pilgrim's plight.

The first and probably most important thing you need to know about Kokopelli is:

He is not someone you want your elementary-school-age kids to investigate.

More about this later. But first, a basic primer.

The image of the humpbacked flute player is one of the most prevalent images in Southwestern rock art.

He is the subject of petroglyphs (which are etched in stone) and pictographs (paintings on stone) in the states of Utah, Colorado, Arizona, and New Mexico. Though there is rock art in all fifty United States, Kokopelli resides only in the Southwest, with the heaviest concentration of figures clustered within a half-day's drive from the Four Corners monument.

It is believed that most of these petroglyphs were made between 200 AD and the mid-1500s, which is when the Spanish first arrived to save native souls. The growth of the Katsina (or Kachina) religion also coincides with the last of the Kokopelli petroglyphs, and flute-player characters were occasionally depicted on pottery during the same period.

Because of the character's chronology and geography, we know that he was carved or drawn primarily by the Anasazi (whose descendants are called Pueblo), Mogollon, Sinagua, and Hohokam peoples—all inhabitants at one time or another of what today are the Four Corners states. The histories and cultures of these groups and others who lived in the region intersected frequently. They shared much more than an interest in the flute-playing rock-art characters.

The second most important thing you need to know about Kokopelli is:

That adorable Native-looking dude you've seen truckin' across T-shirts and ball caps—the one with the horn, the we-be-jammin' posture, and the fashionable dreadlocks tossed ever so jubilantly skyward—probably shouldn't be referred to as "Kokopelli."

I will anyway. Still . . .

Pottery by Melissa Antonio, Acoma Pueblo, New Mexico.
Courtesy of Kennedy Indian Arts and Crafts

"It is such a can of worms," said Barton Wright, a Phoenix author who has written extensively about the Southwest. "The original Kokopelli is so seldom the instigator of what you see today."

Not every humpbacked flute player is "Kokopelli." And, "Kokopelli" doesn't always play a flute.

Here's that can of worms. Sometimes Kokopelli is depicted as severely humpbacked and holding a walking stick. He's also sometimes pictured with knobby knees. The very early stick-figure Kokopellis are often seated and occasionally appear in pairs. And, sometimes, a flute-player is just a flute-player—and not Kokopelli. The "original Kokopelli" referred to by Barton Wright belongs mostly to the Anasazi. According to Peter Pilles, an archaeologist

Belt buckle by James Honyaktewa.
Courtesy of the Albert Long collection

3

for the Coconino National Forest in Arizona, "the specific supernatural figure in Pueblo (Indian) mythology" known today as Kokopelli has a set of very specific attributes: He's playing a flute, he's usually in a prone position facing skyward, he's got a severely humped back, and (keeping things clinical, for the moment) he's macrophallic. One set of Kokopelli authors describes this condition as "phallic in the extreme." Another archaeologist describes his condition as "phallic ostentation."

A Kokopelli character still appears in rituals of Hopi and Zuni, who are Anasazi descendants. Kokopelli appears to be most closely related to the Hopi religion and culture.

The Hohokam were farmers and canal-builders who resided primarily in the Sonoran desert of Arizona and Mexico. Missing from the Hohokam character are the unsightly humped back and the attribute that makes any serious Kokopelli discussion a slightly dicey subject in polite company.

To some, Kokopelli is a rain-making, traveling-salesman love machine. Lately, he's become the region's oldest rock star, a Native deity of good times, the go-to guy for anyone pondering whether or not to order another margarita. And he is quickly becoming one of Southwest's most popular exports.

He is not, however, a good mascot for your sixth-grade daughter's softball team.

4

Romancing the stone idol.

Kokopelli is a leg man.

He is a potent fertility symbol.

Very potent. Kokopelli brings seeds and rain and crops to
the fields, and babies to young maidens. Kokopelli delivers.
Kokopelli is da man. Some of the Native lore about Kokopelli's
sexual escapades would make Casanova blush. But then,
these stories emerged according to the doings of the natural
world versus the needs of man, independent of shame,
which was imported later. Keep that in mind while reading
the next couple of paragraphs.

The image of Kokopelli delivering babies storklike is
one of the more polite ways he may have accomplished the
task of making mothers out of young maidens. One of the
more impolite ways involves an open privy, a trench, and a
set of hollowed out reeds.

It seems that our very social friend became determined
to get better acquainted with a certain young woman of his
village. But she turned him down, or he feared she would,
so he took to observing her habits in order to formulate a
plan. This plan came when he noticed that the young
woman always returned to the same spot to perform her
private duties. Kokopelli dug a tunnel from his house to this
spot, then fitted a number of hollowed reeds together into a
long pipe, and installed it in the tunnel. The next time the
young woman visited the spot where she was accustomed
to so much privacy, well, put your imagination together
with the knowledge of Kokopelli's most legendary—okay,
lengthy—characteristic, and the facts of the young woman's
subsequent pregnancy become clear.

When it comes to this type of legend, the issues of consent vs. nonconsent that our shame-enlightened minds beg
to be addressed just don't apply (see disclaimer regarding
the pinking of Casanova's cheeks, above). But what does
this story tell us about the historical meaning of Kokopelli?
In a world where myths exist to explain the unexplainable,
this one goes a long way to account for the unexplained

pregnancies of any number of innocent young maidens.

It is widely believed that the appearance of the Kokopelli character can be linked to the increasing importance of farming among the Anasazi, the dominant native culture of the Four Corners area. Maize was introduced into the region between 1500 and 900 BC, and gradually changed the Anasazi, originally nomadic and dependent on hunting and gathering, to a settled, comparatively cosmopolitan, agrarian existence. Spirituality in some form had been around for at least five thousand years by now, so the introduction of a powerful fertility figure into the Anasazi mythology at around this time was not without precedence.

It also "makes sense," said James Cunkle, an Arizona archaeologist and author. "When you're sitting in one place tending corn patches and bean patches, you want more fertility, for the sprouts to grow, and you want more children. When you're chasing herd animals, children are a liability. You have to carry them around. When you're sitting in one place, you need them to help tend the fields."

By all indications, Kokopelli delivered results. The people who invoked his spirit became proficient farmers (growing corn, beans, and squash), and the population in the Four Corners region skyrocketed during the years Kokopelli's image was carved into the rocks of the region.

A vessel for ceremonial candy maize.

There were plenty of other seriously endowed rock figures besides Kokopelli, as the phallus so well represented the ancient peoples' intense interest in the subject of fertility. There are also plenty of other kachinas besides Kokopelli that represent fertility in some way. Kokopelli's female counterpart, Kokopellimana, is a good example of both. She also appears on

7

Anasazi pictographs at Kokopelli Cave, Canyon de Chelly National Monument, Arizona.

8

The Hunt, *mild steel,*
by Steve Pevarnik.
This Kokopelli displays
uncharacteristically fine
posture.

the rocks of the Southwest, though not as frequently as da man, and as a kachina she is portrayed during celebrations as man-crazy, aggressively pursuing men to the great amusement of the spectators.

The villages and settlements the Anasazi built—including the cliff dwellings of Mesa Verde National Park and the pueblos of Taos and Chaco Canyon—have stood for centuries. The Anasazi survived climactic changes and severe social upheaval, the European invasion ("Pueblo" is the Spanish word for village-dwellers), and the subsequent ravages of various imported diseases. They mastered a harsh land, and created several distinct languages. They executed the first European they met (the Moor Estebán, a scout for Fray Marcos de Niza's 1539 expedition) when he misbehaved, and, in 1680, conducted the most successful uprising against Europeans by any Southwestern people.

If that cute cat Kokopelli is all you know about the Anasazi, you don't know nearly enough.

And that's just about all we really "know" about Kokopelli. Now comes some of the interesting gab that's out there on the subject. Call it speculation, extrapolation, interpretation, or just plain zany guesswork—Kokopelli has generated all kinds of interesting theories. For example:

Kokopelli didn't necessarily use his flute—if it was a flute—to make pleasant music.

9

If it wasn't a flute, maybe it was a whistle or a mechanism used ceremonially, such as a pipe, with which Kokopelli floated prayers toward the skies.

But the evidence points to flute. Bone and wood flutes aplenty have been found at Anasazi burial sites. The music made from the scale of notes they play—A#, C, C#, D, F, G, A—likely accompanied dance and ritual. Music—along with other arts; the Anasazi were expert pot makers and textile craftspeople—was obviously important to ancient native cultures.

Other clues that seem to substantiate the flute theory are associations that have survived in present-day rituals. On the Hopi mesas, the Kokopelli kachina is not a flute player but he borrows a flute from another kachina during certain dances, and among the Hopi the flute is associated with the growth of spring vegetation.

At Zuni, two figures that are associated with fertility play flutes. The Zuni sometimes call Kokopelli by the name of the flute used by their rain priests; they also say that Kokopelli himsef was a rain priest and that his presence on rocks throughout the Southwest is meant to bring rain to the region.

Among Native American cultures in general, the use of a flute is allied with wooing maidens, attracting sheep for

A Hopi Kokopelli Kachina by Tino Youvella.

hunting, bringing rain and promoting the growth of flowers, and announcing one's arrival at an unfamiliar village.

If Kokopelli was modeled, as some believe, on an itinerant trader, the flute would have signaled a village that the approaching figure was friendly and had something to sell. The practice continues in modern times, in the form of mobile lunch wagons with horns that play "La Cucaracha."

Rock art is probably not "art."

The study of rock art uncovers far more questions than answers, making it impossible to know the real purpose of the pecking and painting. A small percentage of petroglyphs appear to be mere doodling. Other etchings could have been a form of journalism, the CNN of the day, crude recordings of an event. Others appear to be trail markers. But the majority of petroglyphs are believed to have ritualistic purposes.

"It's sympathetic magic," said anthropologist Cunkle. "Shamans creating images to make things happen."

Surviving tribes still consider petroglyph sites to be sacred.

11

Kokopelli might have been based on a real person, or people.

He's a hunter, warrior, musician, trickster, fertility god, or insect. Maybe Kokopelli was a traveling salesman. Considering his prominence on the marquees of so many contemporary knickknack shops, the Kokopelli-as-trader legend has great credence based on staying power alone.

One popular theory: Kokopelli was a puchteca— a traveling trader from the Aztec or Mayan cultures of Mesoamerica who appeared in the Southwest at about the same time the rock art depictions of Kokopelli did. There is evidence that the region's various tribes interacted not only with one another, but with visitors from the south as well. The puchteca played a flute and enjoyed the reputation of a sailor or a traveling salesman: a girl in every village, so to speak.

Flute player petroglyph at Crack-in-Rock site, Wupatki National Monument, Arizona.

"There were probably real Kokopellis running around with backpacks full of goodies, up from Central America," said James Cunkle. "They were trading probably for turquoise." The goodies-in-return, Cunkle said, likely included exotic birds, copper bells, and "all kinds of wonderful things made in Central America."

If Kokopelli's true-life model was a traveling trader from the south, his influence on the Anasazi was profound. In addition to the all-important corn crop, the use of cotton for garments, some pottery designs, agricultural techniques (such as irrigation), and the bow-and-arrow are some of the many elements of Anasazi life that were imported from Mexico and/or South America.

The traveling-salesman theory in part explains Kokopelli's hump: maybe it was a sack for carrying goods.

Or maybe the sack was filled with rainbows.

It is either a hump or a sack, but let's say it is probably a sack or bag full of happy stuff. According to Hopi lore, Kokopelli's sack is filled with buckskin, which he stitches into gala garments and footwear for a village's maidens. This is the Kokopelli-as-fashion-designer myth, in which he uses his wares to seduce young girls. Appropriately enough, another myth says the sack is full of babies, which Kokopelli, um, distributes to young women.

If Kokopelli was a deity or an envoy between man and the gods, as some believe he was, his hump/sack could have been filled with seeds, mist, and clouds—even a rainbow. Rain was an obvious preoccupation for the Anasazi. Other kachinas

Kokopelli, *hand-forged steel with patina, by Dutch Walker. Courtesy of New West Galleries*

12

have been known to carry things on their backs, and humps
have been attributed with supernatural powers.

*Some of Kokopelli's odder attributes have been
explained as symptoms of disease.*

A malformed spine, knobby knees, and perpetual erec-
tion, or priapism (from Priapus, a Greek and Roman fertility
god), are all symptoms of Pott's disease, a form of tubercu-
losis that plagued the Pueblo Indians. There is no account-
ing, in this explanation, for Kokopelli's wild hair.

13

Maybe Kokopelli's wild hair is antennae.

Some Kokopelli petroglyphs have been interpreted as
insects.

One bug frequently mentioned as the possible model for
Kokopelli is the robber fly. And fittingly so, considering the
robber fly's propensity to furiously copulate with other robber
flies—when it is not stealing their larvae. Among some Hopi,
Kokopelli is a Robber Fly kachina.

The locust and dragonfly are candidates as well. The
musical patron of the Hopi flute societies, the locust was
sent ahead as a scout when the Hopi emerged into the
upper world, and locusts play the flute to melt snow. The
dragonfly has the appearance of being humpbacked and its
mating habits are appropriately rigorous.

Then again, maybe it's ceremonial headgear.

If it is hair, Kokopelli pre-figures the heavy metal bands
of the late 1980s by a full millennium. But it is probably
feathers and stuff.

So concludes your Kokopelli primer. Graduate school
starts on the next page.

Kokopelli gets pole position on Central Avenue in Phoenix.
Copper medallion by Howard Sice.

CHAPTER TWO

ADVANCED KOKOPELLI

Although it is clearly not grounded in the objective truth of what we know about the character's roots, the Kokopelli craze is fueled by some powerful magic. There's something cool, catchy, kitschy about Kokopelli. And, as we've learned, something quite mysterious.

One day during the research phase of my personal Kokopelli quest, I was driving on Central Avenue, Phoenix's main thoroughfare. Inching through traffic, pondering all I had learned, Kokopelli—or whoever—spoke to me again.

"Yo, professor," said the voice. "Pull that sled over."

After signaling and dutifully checking to make sure the next lane was clear, I did. A few years ago, the City of Phoenix redecorated its main drag with lovely desert land-scaping and tasteful light poles. From each pole hangs a turquoise-colored disk. Carved into each turquoise disc or riveted to it is a petroglyph-looking design.

As fate would have it, I found myself parked directly beneath a light-pole disc decorated with the image of a certain humpbacked flute player.

"Ready for your mid-terms, Poindexter?" said the voice.

"Not exactly," I said. "I have so much more to learn."

"Word," he said.

There were several long seconds of silence.

"Well, what next?" I said.

There were several more long seconds of silence.

"Road trip," he said.

Jammin' under the Kokopelli dome.

15

The two-hour drive to Sedona, Arizona—a Southwestern tourist mecca on the front lines of the contemporary Kokopelli invasion—gave me some time for further Kokopelli contemplation.

Why him? Why now?

It seemed highly unlikely that the folks buying all of those Kokopelli oven mitts know many of the intimate details of the real Kokopelli. (You know . . . *it?*) Or, for that matter, care very much that the guy they're calling Kokopelli isn't really the true Kokopelli.

The contemporary Kokopelli figure, though considerably less threatening than most of his hard-rock predecessors, nonetheless conveys something appealing and powerful. His posture, his hair (or whatever), his wailing horn, all combine into a unified life-of-the-party image. Mix in just a little of his background, and Kokopelli's appeal grows more understandable.

Be he traveling salesman, itinerant musician, or godlike fertility figure, he's certainly got lots of modern-day models. Saxist Kenny G, Bob and/or Ziggy Marley, Jimmy Buffett, and Jethro Tull's Ian Anderson (for the Renaissance Festival crowd) all cast a Kokopelli-like shadow when the light's just right. I see lots of Kokopelli in Keith Richards, too. And, of course, there's blues diva Koko Taylor.

16

Ancient fertility gods need hobbies, too.

For all our adulation of the carefree lives of musicians and entertainers, however, who among us would want that life for our children? Is a transient, promiscuous, responsibility-free life to be admired, desired, emulated? Most sober, sensible citizens would say, "Yes, I'd trade my life as a (your sad, boring life here) for Keith Richards' life as a carousing, groupie-groping rock musician in a heartbeat. Where do I sign?" Yet, hardly a day goes by when you don't read about some musician getting thrown off of a commercial airliner for public drunkenness. Or throwing perfectly good TV sets off of a hotel balcony. Or just throwing up.

Since the true Kokopelli's facility for fertility has been mostly edited out of his contemporary manifestation, that doesn't seem to be a big part of his appeal. Or does it? Procreation and its pregame show remain preoccupations in modern life. Next to daytime TV talk shows and annual analysis of the Super Bowl commercials, sex is still the most interesting thing going. And, as you've been warned, just a little digging into the Kokopelli story reveals that he's got substantial sexual subtext.

But it would appear to be impolite, politically incorrect subtext. Though the Pueblo Indians had to be taught the concept of sexual shame—first by the conquering Spaniards, then priests, then tourists—Western civilization has long

17

Kokopelli sez: Accessorize!

been well acquainted with the subject. In one Hopi dance ritual, Kokopelli has been depicted by a dancer who actually bared his genitals. In later renditions of the same dance, a colorful gourd was substituted for the offending, um, equipment.

Various interpretations depict Kokopelli as an unrelenting Lothario and a bit of a cad, a guy who's capable of magically impregnating maidens without their consent. Then again, maybe his appeal has less to do with the Kokopelli figure itself—and his sometimes salacious legacy—than the region he represents.

"Really," says Phoenix author Barton Wright, who's made a long-term study of Kokopelli, "it's just like the howling coyote. Everybody gets hooked on one thing and it becomes popular and you see it appearing everywhere until it gets worn out. These various forms of iconography catch the attention of people and simply become cliches. The term 'Kokopelli,' the term 'Kachina,' the howling coyote, the roadrunner—the whole batch of them at one time or another has gone through this process. It's the

Get a Kokopelli tattoo and become a walking petroglyph. Courtesy of Burly Fish Tattoo and Body Piercing

idea of the Great Southwest [embodied in the coyote that attracts the keepsake dollar], not the coyote itself."

The Kokopelli craze likely "started with this romantic idea of a mysterious individual playing a flute," Wright continued. "The mystique of the original thought is still there, so people use it as a symbol for everything under the sun."

Consider a typical Southwestern tourist itinerary: With a headful of imagery from half-remembered Hollywood movies, a visitor touches down in Phoenix, Albuquerque, or Las Vegas. After a few days in a posh resort, chain hotel, or glass-and-steel pyramid, our guests load onto a large bus for a whirlwind tour of the Grand Canyon, Monument Valley, Sedona, or Santa Fe. They hit a scenic overlook or two, swarm the gift shops, grab a quick Diet Coke—oops, time's up. Back on the bus, folks!

A Kokopelli keepsake, no matter what it really means, is as close as most visitors get to the Southwest's ancient, eternal spirit.

And how big of a drag would modern life be without a little cultural appropriation? Think of all the glorious stuff that exists as we know it because someone, somewhere, swiped a piece of someone else's culture, then put a little commercial topspin on it. Why, there'd be no rock 'n' roll, no Bud Light, no bottle rockets. No California rolls, no ballpark

Kokopelli Stripe, painted ponderosa pine, copyright © by Dan and Peg O'Leary. Courtesy of Zonies Galleria

19

nachos, no karaoke. The list—Chinese checkers…toaster waffles…Zydeco…French fries—goes on. Even the ancient Anasazi borrowed from neighboring cultures.

Not to excuse the exploitation of long-exploited people, but the quote-Kokopelli-unquote most people know and love, who's barely a distant relative of the fellow carved on Anasazi rocks, can't be a truly harmful character. A little disrespectful, maybe. Rowdy, sure. Insulting? Harmful? Depends on who you're asking. Some contemporary Native Americans and other sensitive observers object to the commercialization of such a sacred figure. Then again, some don't.

The appropriation of Native icons is nothing new. The Phoenix phone book lists nearly sixty businesses named "Kachina" (compared with just five, so far, that use "Kokopelli"), which some Natives would say is akin to similarly employing another sacred name. Would you buy a used car from Jesus Christ Cadillac?

"I am sensitive to the Native Americans [who object to the Kokopelli boom]," said archaeologist James Cunkle, who also runs a business that uses Kokopelli's name in its title. "But most of the Native Americans [who object] have no connection to the Pueblo Indians. Only the Hopi and Zuni can say, 'Hey, that's our mythology.'" Otherwise, concludes Cunkle, "It's like me complaining about people using the images of King David or the Romans."

Gloria Lomahaftewa, a Hopi who serves as the assistant to the director of Native American Relations of the Heard Museum in Phoenix, says she has "mixed feelings" about the commercial appropriation of a figure her people still hold sacred.

"What Kokopelli signifies within Hopi and the figure that is being portrayed are totally different," she said. "The twisting of what Kokopelli means is making it an insignificant figure within American society."

20

Rabbi-pelli: Sedona artist Robert Shields (of "Shields and Yarnell" fame), has incorporated a Star of David on this Kokopelli pendant.

Someone's dreaming of a Kokopelli Christmas.

21

Peter Welsh, an Arizona State University anthropology professor and director of the Deer Valley Rock Art Center in Phoenix, said he wouldn't wear a garment printed with the Kokopelli figure. The gift shop in the Rock Art Center sells various souvenirs emblazoned with real petroglyph designs, but no Kokopellis, mostly because there are no Kokopelli glyphs on the center's grounds.

"I find myself being tremendously ambivalent about the transferal of what strikes me as site-specific art to all kinds of portable media," said Welsh, noting the proliferation of a "whole constellation of images, some of which are Kokopelli in its mythological aspects."

It is a proliferation he is not entirely comfortable with. "It is, it seems, at one level a form of appreciation," he said. "It's hard for all of us to sort out where appreciation begins and appropriation ends. These images are as much, if not more, a part of today for the casual visitors as they are a part of the past, so people are fully prepared to make of them what they want."

Victor Gonzalez, a Pasqua-Yaqui and tour guide at the Rock Art Center, likens the Kokopelli figure to Santa Claus—a beloved character in many cultures whose meaning is slightly different for each. The analogy even incorporates the hump-as-sack theory, not to mention the character's surging commerciality.

Which puts Kokopelli—whoever he is—in pretty cool company.

Entering the greater Sedona area, I drove past the Kokopelli Inn (complete with iron depictions of Mr. K. welded into the balcony railing), past an uptown bike shop (decorated with a gang of mountain-biking Kokopellis), and into a restaurant parking lot. Dylan's was the name of the place. A giant Kokopelli stood over the entrance. Across the street, two more giant Koko-cutouts flanked the sign above a large art gallery.

I drove on through Sedona, stopping in the heart of the tourist district, in front of a store emblazoned with several large Kokopellis. Inside was displayed a forest of Koko-keepsakes. An array of ceramic tile depicted him as a tennis player and a golfer. One tile showed a red pickup truck full of little Kokopellis. Next door, Kokopelli jewelry. Next door to that, Kokopelli books. A little farther down the street, Kokopelli garb. The clothing store carried several T-shirts and a half-dozen different ballcaps, each featuring a distinctive Koko-pose. One cap actually carried the words, "We be jammin'."

22

A series of ceramic tiles depicting Kokopelli's active lifestyle.

Pilgrims welcome.

23

"What is it that people see in you?" I asked the cap. "Is it your devil-may-care pose? Your unruly locks? Or are they all Kenny G fans?"

Surrounded by tourists from many nations, I addressed the hat unselfconsciously. Sedona has seen far stranger

behavior. Still, one of the visitors heard something he recognized.

"Kenny G—Ya!" he said, in a German or Swedish or Latvian accent, giving me a double thumbs-up.

Desperate for answers, I ignored him.

"What do you mean to these people?" I said to the hat. "You're becoming the Izod alligator of the late twentieth century, a regional phenomenon breaking big. Everybody's doing the Koko-motion."

Silence.

"Why you?" I said to the hat. "Why now?"

"Don't ask me," he said. "Why not ask the people?"

Silence.

"Ya," I said. "Why not?"

A taste of the (very) old Southwest, courtesy of the Kokopelli winery in Willcox, Arizona.

CHAPTER THREE

CUCKOO FOR KOKOPELLI

Kokopelli's commercial afterlife is one of the breakaway economic success stories of our time. Businesses in more than twenty states carry his name. Type Kokopelli into a World Wide Web search engine, and more than 1,200 "hits" surface.

It's no big surprise that phone books in Sedona, Scottsdale, Santa Fe, Aspen, Vail, and Durango carry Kokopelli listings. But Baltimore, Maryland? Canoga Park, California? Hinsdale, Illinois? A Canadian youth choir and a New Jersey rock band have adopted the name. Hair salons in Denver and Marietta, Georgia, have, too. There are horse stables, construction companies, and two golf courses (one in Illinois) named for Kokopelli. David Amram has composed a three-suite symphony named for Kokopelli. A self-storage lot in Mescalero, New Mexico, is called Kokopelli Pods. Willcox, Arizona, has the Kokopelli Winery. Off-road bicycle enthusiasts travel to Colorado to ride the scenic Kokopelli Trail. There are countless restaurants, motels, art galleries, jewelry stores, and gift shops called Kokopelli. There is a Kokopelli Caffe, Kafe, Kafe & Bakery, Kaffe 'n' Deli, and Coffee Kaboose.

We are cuckoo for Kokopelli.

I spoke with several business owners around the country who've made the Koko-connection. Without exception, they were pleasant, polite, and more than willing to share their own Kokopelli-discovery stories. Clearly, there's something about the humpbacked flute player that attracts nice folks. This is, perhaps, a clue to the true spirit of Kokopelli.

Let a traveling salesman hold your cash.

Picnic with a petroglyph at Kokopelli's Kitchen.

26

KOKOPELLI'S KITCHEN GOURMET SPECIALTY FOODS

St. Johns, Arizona

Kokopelli's Kitchen Gourmet Specialty Foods is a purveyor of meals that Kokopelli himself might have sampled. Based in Phoenix and St. Johns, Arizona, the company markets packages of ingredients that can be made into soups, stews, breads, cocoas, and salsas. The goods are typically sold in gift shops and other tourist magnets. The recipes were developed at the White Mountain Archaeological Center based on the culinary traditions of the region's prehistoric natives, as well as later Spanish and pioneer settlers. And here's the best part: Proceeds from the food line help support Raven Site Ruin, an active pueblo "dig" between St. Johns and Springerville, near the Arizona–New Mexico border.

"It's an expensive proposition to keep a staff there tending to things, keeping things stabilized, and keeping the fencing up," said Carol Cunkle, half of the husband-and-wife team that operates the Kitchen and oversees work at Raven Site. "The site was being pot-hunted" as recently as the early 1980s, Cunkle said. "It was literally being destroyed by backhoes."

Today, visitors can participate in the excavation work at Raven Site, or tour nearby petroglyph sites. A few years ago, the Cunkles made a find that gave their contemporary cuisine business a direct link to the past.

"When we were working on the ruin, we discovered a bowl of beans in a dry cave," James Cunkle said. "We dated the bowl at AD 1100. Here were these beans, sitting in a dry cave, sitting patiently and waiting for sunlight and moisture."

The Cunkles sent some of the beans to researchers in Tucson, who are working to preserve the genetic stock of native seeds. Some of the rest, they planted.

"They grew into a five-foot-high bush with flowers the hummingbirds loved," said James Cunkle. The plant's fruit, though, wasn't such an aesthetic success. Or, at least the Cunkles couldn't devise a palatable way to prepare the crop for contemporary consumption.

"I couldn't cook 'em," said James Cunkle. "They were terrible."

Carol's recipes for the Kokopelli's Kitchen line have proven much more successful. "Carol, who's a very good chef, experimented with all kinds of things the prehistoric Indians may have made," said James Cunkle. "We know they made a lot of soupy things—you never find plates, it's all bowls and jars—and they made bread to dip into the soups."

The Cunkles first test-marketed their food packets in the small gift shop at Raven Site. "We said, 'Well, let's see if it works,'" said Carol Cunkle. "We don't get much traffic up here, just seven thousand visitors a year. But they bought it, and we thought, 'Maybe we have something here.'"

KOKOPELLI COFFEE AND TEA

Cleveland, Ohio

Rick Sheehan, proprietor of two Kokopelli Coffee and Tea shops in the Cleveland area, first encountered Kokopelli on a visit to one of the petroglyph sites near Albuquerque. He adopted the character for his business mascot after an unpleasant breakup with a partner in an earlier coffee-house venture.

"I didn't work for about six months after breaking up with my partner," he said. "It was a six-month headache. Toward the end of the six months, we came up with the Kokopelli name, and things turned around for me."

Southwestern iconography isn't an everyday sight in Cleveland. At first, "a lot of people thought it was my last name," Sheehan said. "Like anything else, you've got to educate them. We have a little something about Kokopelli on our carry-out menu."

Pre-Kokopelli, Sheehan and his wife "were trying to get pregnant." Post-Kokopelli, they've successfully adopted, and the coffee-house business is good.

"My luck has turned around," he said. "We've got a couple of stores in the Cleveland area, a warehouse, and a nineteen-month-old now. I had a little bad luck. Kokopelli's kind of a positive character, kind of a good-luck charm. It's definitely been good luck."

KOKOPELLI PRODUCTS

Kalispell, Montana

John Werre and his wife fell in love with Kokopelli while traveling the Southwest on business. "We both felt very comfortable down there, like we'd been there before," he said.

The Werres run two businesses in Kalispell, Montana, using the Kokopelli Products name. One business markets "health products, herbs, and that sort of thing," said Werre.

The other specializes in custom gear for rifles.

"Kokopelli seems to be one of the more interesting characters as far as Pueblo Indian deities go," said Werre. "We just kind of hooked up on him."

Set your table with the Mambo King of the Mesas.

29

KOKOPELLI'S
Midland, Michigan

Lanny Dexter wanted to bring Southwestern cuisine to Midland, Michigan, but was stuck for a name until a pal in Sedona, Arizona, suggested a certain humpbacked icon.

Kokopelli's features Mexican border specialties and a big list of microbrews. In addition to the typical hair-tossing, flute-tooting Kokopelli figure, Dexter's place mats show the figure pounding a tom-tom and delivering a tray full of food.

"Midland, Michigan, is about five years behind California," said Dexter. "Southwestern food is coming up now through the bigger cities in Michigan. I'm about three years ahead of myself. The name is unique, out-of-the-ordinary, and people say, 'What the hell is that?' I get a lot of calls saying, 'Is this an Italian place?'"

KOKOPELLI CONTEMPORARY GALLERY
Key West, Florida

Kokopelli Contemporary Gallery doesn't specialize in Southwestern keepsakes, but the Duval Street gift shop in Key West, Florida, does carry a few select items.

"We sell the Kokopelli earrings and pendants, hundreds of 'em," said owner Jerry Beesinger. "Key West is very big with Europeans. The Germans are just crazy about Kokopelli."

Beesinger and his wife, Louise, have Albuquerque roots, so the Kokopelli tie-in was a natural—even in Key West's Caribbean setting.

"We wanted a catchy name with a Southwestern flair," Jerry Beesinger said. "We figured nobody would know what Kokopelli meant." So, a drawing of the character and a brief version of the Kokopelli legend is printed on the store's business card. "We go through six hundred cards a month," he said. "These people just go nuts over it."

KOKOPELLI NEW MEDIA DEVELOPMENT
New York, New York

Glen Lipka made his first contact with Kokopelli on a cross-country trip after college graduation. He now runs the New York City design firm called Kokopelli New Media Development, an Internet consultant.

"All along the way, we had been buying little mementos of each city," he said. "In Albuquerque, I bought a little stylized Kokopelli figure, put a key-chain loop through it, and have used it as a key chain ever since. When we founded the company, and were thinking of a lot of different names, I woke up in the middle of the night and thought, 'Kokopelli.' It hadn't occurred to me before that, but it really embodied all the things we wanted the company we were building to be. It was fun for us, and Kokopelli was a fun character. We wanted to make a lot of money, so the fertility aspect was important. And, on the World Wide Web, you want an icon that's very 'clickable.' The symbol is easy to animate. It's something that every single one of our clients have asked about. It's a conversation starter, an ice-breaker."

KOKOPELLI ENTERPRISES

Jackson, Mississippi

31

Riley Kelley answered the phone when I called a Jackson, Mississippi, business listing for Kokopelli.

"Is this Kokopelli Enterprises?" I asked.

"Depends," said Kelley, wary of capitol-seeking entrepreneurs.

As it turned out, Kelley is a certified public accountant who once worked "as a public practitioner in a small shop in Santa Fe," he said. That's where he first learned of the Kokopelli figure.

"It's been good luck for me for years," he said. "There are Kokopelli reliefs hanging in our house, up above the fireplace, and there are Kokopellis in our courtyard, tiptoeing through the tulips. My wife and all my daughters have Kokopelli charms and necklaces and earrings. They say they wear them to keep their karma charged."

Not to mention their bank accounts.

"Kokopelli Enterprises Limited is really a closely held corporation I established about two years ago, really for my children," he said. "It's really just an investment corporation. I put a fair chunk of change in there and told them, 'It's really y'all's money.'"

And, as a father of three girls, Kelley is not unaware of Kokopelli's power as a fertility figure.

"The name has been dear to my heart for many years," he said. "The name itself, and what it means, should give them some degree of direction."

32

Discover the cool sounds of Kokopelli Records.

KOKOPELLI RECORDS
Santa Fe, New Mexico

Before co-founding his jazz-based record label, Jim Geisler worked in nightclubs and as a concert promoter.

"Primarily rock 'n' roll," he said. "You know the saying, 'If it's too loud, you're too old.' I realized I was."

He co-founded Kokopelli Records with Herbie Mann, a veteran jazz flute player and world-music maven. He and Geisler have since parted ways, but the Santa Fe–based label continues to produce jazz discs for the world.

"There has been good and bad in terms of having the name," said Geisler. "Without Herbie's involvement, it sounds as if we should be doing Native American–New Age kinds of music. While we do some of that, it's not our primary focus. That's been a little problematic. Internationally, it's kind of helped. You get over into Italy, and they go, 'Oooo, American Indians. Oooo, American jazz.'"

KOKOPELLI'S PIZZA INTERNATIONAL
Fairfax, Virginia

In several locations in the mid-Atlantic states, Kokopelli delivers. A ten-store pizza chain based in Fairfax, Virginia, Kokopelli's Pizza International was founded by partners who have Southwestern roots.

33

"He's on all our boxes, right in the middle," said Steve Quinn, one of the partners. "We use a cutout shape of Kokopelli for a refrigerator magnet. He's on all our napkins, and all our uniforms.

"The Kokopelli figure itself represents a free-and-easy lifestyle, running around the desert playing the flute. We don't play up the fertility aspect."

Kokopelli's Pizza specializes in carryout and delivery pizza made with top-quality ingredients, including a sprinkle of Southwestern lore.

"They're fascinated with that back here," Quinn said. "When they start finding out about it, they ask a lot of questions. It's been kind of a fascination [for customers]," Quinn continued. "People in the East think it's an Italian name. That's fine with us."

KOKOPELLI
Edmond, Oklahoma

Karen Marquis and Mary Smith learned about Kokopelli from a customer of their Edmond, Oklahoma, import shop. When the time came to open up a clothing store for women, the name seemed like a good fit.

"We were kind of intrigued with it, and decided to name the store Kokopelli," Marquis said. "We thought it would bring us good luck and fortune."

So far, so Kokopacetic. There are now four Kokopelli clothing stores—in Edmond, Norman, and Oklahoma City, Oklahoma, and Fayetteville, Arkansas.

"We have women's clothing and casual, soft clothes, and we have kind of a Santa Fe look to our store, with little adobe-looking arches," Marquis said. "We don't sell a lot of Southwestern styles, but sell lots of cottons and natural fibers and things."

34

Like many of the businesspeople who've adopted Kokopelli as a mascot, Marquis and her partner have de-emphasized one of the traditional character's more prominent characteristics.

"When we were trying to find out about Kokopelli, people would tell us different things," Marquis said. "We heard about the fertility aspect a lot, and we wanted to make sure that he wasn't a mysterious person who hid in dark caves and jumped out at unknowing people."

Besides, she added, "We don't need the fertility part. My partner and I already have a couple of kids apiece."

KOKOPELLI'S CAVE BED AND BREAKFAST
Farmington, New Mexico

A short drive from Mesa Verde National Monument, Kokopelli's Cave Bed & Breakfast offers visitors a contemporary cliff-dwelling experience. This B&B is a one-bedroom cave home carved into a cliff above the La Plata River, just north of Farmington, New Mexico. Its 1,650 square feet of living space is carpeted, has a microwave-equipped kitchen, hot and cold running water, and a flagstone hot tub.

Opened in June 1997, and so far marketed only via a World Wide Web page, Kokopelli's Cave was an immediate success.

"It's been incredible," said Bruce Black, proprietor. "I have done zero advertising, and have had solid bookings."

Originally designed as a unique office for Black's business (he's a consulting geologist), the cave was a father-son project for Black and his son, also named Bruce.

"I was born and raised in New Mexico, and have been surrounded by the Indian culture all my life," said Bruce Sr. "I love the architecture, particularly of the Anasazi, the Ancient Ones. Kokopelli is pecked all over the Southwest, a figure that shows up everywhere. Nobody really knows what he meant. The people who put him up there are long gone. From my standpoint, I've always thought he was a cute, mythical creature. I use him for my logo. He's kind of a pied-piper figure. He sure is bringing in the business."

From coast to coast and all around the world, the spirit of the humpbacked flute player has captured the hearts and cash registers of thousands of pleasant folks. As we've discovered, the character who's leading the commercial conga line is, at best, a distant relative of the true Kokopelli. The only opinion missing so far is his.

He's seen fire, he's seen rain. . . .
by Iron Craft, courtesy of Zonies Galleria

CHAPTER FOUR

INTERVIEW WITH A KOKOPELLI

On the subject of ancient mythological beings, research and fieldwork get you only so far. After exploring all of the popular Kokopelli texts, surveying his modern-day kingdom, and interviewing some of his acolytes, it was finally time to go directly to the source.

For most folks, contacting an old-timer like Kokopelli would be a tall order. But I live in the Southwest, where melding the present with the distant past is a bit of a cottage industry. Sensitive seers in Sedona and Santa Fe summon ancient Egyptians and the like all the time. Arranging for a personal appearance by Kokopelli couldn't be all that hard. After all, we'd been trading psychic voicemail for awhile. It was high time for some face time.

I started the process by traveling to the corner convenience market. There, I purchased a twelve-pack of a fermented beverage known to enhance certain rituals. I also secured a bag of snack chips made from indigenous maize—likely a staple of the real Kokopelli's household—and, of course, some delicious salsa. Once home, I lit a fire in the fireplace, turned the lights down low, and thought ancient thoughts. Soon, Kokopelli appeared to me.

He spoke in the same gruff, smoky voice I'd been hearing in my head, and cackled when he laughed. He looked just like the humpbacked flute player of the petroglyphs. Kokopelli seemed to be of average height, not counting his tall headdress. For most of our conversation, he slumped in an easy chair on the opposite side of my living room.

. . . He's seen chip-and-dip parties he thought would never end.

Occasionally, he would take a long, contemplative puff on
what appeared to be a pipe. The room was dark, so it was
hard to see what he was wearing, if anything. Something, I
could only hope.

The following is a transcript of our discussion.

Dave: Kokopelli, is that you?

Kokopelli: Maybe. Who's asking?

D: I am but a humble pilgrim, searching for the true
spirit of Kokopelli.

K: Oh, brother.

38

D: Well, are you Kokopelli? The humpbacked flute
player? The cliff-dwelling Casanova? The Mambo King
of the mesas?

K: You were expecting maybe Dean Martin?

D: Wow. It is you.

K: Wow is right.

D: I have so many questions.

K: Fire away, pilgrim.

D: Were you—are you—a man or a god?

K: What man does not believe that he is a bit of both?

D: So you were a man.

K: That's not what I said.

D: Well, which is it?

K: It's not that simple.

D: Did you ever walk the Earth in human form?

**K: Oh, sure. All the time. That is, when I wasn't fly-
ing around in my spaceship.**

**(He laughs.) Who knew that rock artists would be
watching? They were the paparazzi of their day, I'm
telling you.**

D: How would you describe your state of being at the
moment?

**K: Well, obviously I'm a deity now. In fact, Bacchus,
Aphrodite, Jim Morrison, and I were in the middle of a
very hot hand of bridge when you summoned me here.**

D: Sorry.

K: No problem. That Bacchus, what a pistol!

D: The place where you are—what's it like?

K: Oh, no. No, you don't. I'm not going to spill all the afterlife details. There's a non-disclosure clause in the contract you sign when you become a deity. It's boilerplate, pretty standard stuff. But humankind isn't going to ever get any answers to that question, so just give it up, Bob Woodward.

D: Do you live in the clouds?

K: Okay, here's a hint. The only character here who's even remotely cherubic-looking is Count Basie.

D: So, you're in the musicians' wing of heaven?

K: You might say that. But I've got visiting privileges in some of the other sectors, too. Man—or god—does not live by harp music alone.

D: I don't see a flute. Where's your flute?

K: I'm semi-retired at the moment, but there's been some talk of a VH1 special. Maybe a package tour with Bob Marley and Louis Armstrong. That would be a gas.

D: Where you are—is it nice?

K: Let's put it this way. The all-you-can-eat buffet never runs out of shrimp.

D: Just for the sake of argument, let's say that you once visited Earth in human form.

K: Oh, a game. I love games. Sure, let's pretend. . . .

D: What was your role here on Earth? There are lots of theories. . . .

K: Air conditioning repair . . . Square-dance caller . . . Chairman of the House Ways and Means Committee . . .

39

Raku Kokopelli by Judy Kampa. Courtesy of Zonies Galleria

Kokopelli mural in Parks, Arizona, by Loona Otero.

D: Seriously, though . . .

K: These questions aren't exactly going to get you into our media wing. Charles Kuralt is the new membership chairman, and he's got pretty high standards.

D: Were you a trader? A trickster? A freelance agronomist?

K: (Singing) I've been a pauper, a poet, a pawn, and a king. . . .

D: What did you carry in your backpack? Or was it a hump? Or did you suffer, as some have suggested, from some form of crippling disease?

K: Those are all correct. And none of them is correct. I've been advised to remain enigmatic. Valhalla is full of expert spin doctors.

D: Okay, okay. Let's talk about your flute for a minute instead.

K: It's your nickel. Summoning a spirit stills costs a nickel, right?

D: First off, is it really a flute? There's some disagreement.

K: Well, it sure isn't a telescope.

D: Some people believe it's a dart gun, or maybe just a big nose.

K: No, it is a flute. Musician has been a great gig for a long, long time.

D: What does your music sound like?

K: Based on what I've heard, the New Age guys have it about right. Very soothing. It's good hot tub music. That's what the ladies tell me, at least.

D: And that stuff on your head?

K: What can I say. That's my 'do. You ever have a bad-hair day?

D: Sure.

K: Well, I'm having a bad-hair millennium.

D: Otherwise, how accurate are the petroglyph representations of you?

K: Considering what the artists had to work with—rocks—they're not bad. I'd say they're most accurate in one, um, personal regard. Nothing else really matters, if you know what I'm saying.

D: Um, I think I do. Maybe we should move on.

K: Maybe we should.

D: Have you been following how your image has become such a hot commercial property?

K: At last! A relevant question!

D: Does it bother you at all that you've become the Acme of our time? All kinds of businesses have appropriated your name and image. Even golf courses.

K: Look, one of my jobs on Earth was trader. I'm a free-market kind of guy. I'm more than happy to help the small businessman make a buck.

D: Your image here has become kind of an all-purpose party animal. In fact, you rival the howling coyote as the good-time ambassador of the Southwest.

K: You mean that mangy mutt Butch? He had a good run. Lately, though, his big excitement is barking at the meter-reader.

D: So, you don't have any problems hawking chimichangas?

K: Nah, not at all. People sometimes get the impression that pre-Columbian life was a big drag. You know: grind some corn, build a cliff dwelling, throw a pot. Not so! We had dances, we had music. Lately, I've begun to feel a little like one of the Gabor sisters, but I suppose there

42

Kokopelli: Cultivation of Soul, *painted rusted metal, by Gina Designs. Courtesy of Zonies Galleria*

Kokopelli with Kolorfusion Finish, *metal, by Jim L. Ivins Copyright © by Lazart Productions, Inc. Courtesy of Native Spirit*

could be worse feelings. Have another margarita, Earthlings, dance the Kokopelli dance while you can.

D: No hard feelings whatsoever?

K: I don't let it bug me. It's next to impossible to collect royalties where I live. Believe me, I had our legal department look into it.

D: There's a legal department there?

K: Yeah, but it's little. Clarence Darrow and Abe Lincoln are the only two who've made it so far. Are we about finished here? I don't want to miss Happy Hour.

D: Yes, I think we're done. Thanks for the visit. See you 'round.

K: Ain't that the truth?

Pull up a rocker and join the band. Steel Kokopelli by Steve Pevarnik.

EPILOGUE

So concluded my conversation with Kokopelli.

I haven't had a discussion with a ballcap or lamp post
in weeks, but he's still a big part of my life, as I suspect he
will remain for quite some time. Kokopelli's playful posture
and beguiling subtext will continue to enchant
Southwestern tourists and locals alike. He's our oldest rock
star, the pre-Columbian Coolio, the charismatic headliner of
Mesoamerican Bandstand. As the patron saint of hospitality
in the Four Corners states, he's the guy to call when you
want to party like it's 999.

If you want to learn more about Kokopelli (especially
some of the racy stuff I've left out) and the people who
carved his image into Southwestern stone, a short reading
list follows.

And, should you someday find
yourself sitting in heavy traffic on
Central Avenue in Phoenix, keep an
eye on those lamp posts.

Kokopelli delivers.

SELECTED BIBLIOGRAPHY

Kokopelli: Ancient Myth, Modern Icon, by Wayne Glover. Camelback/Canyonlands Publishing, Bellemont, Arizona, 1995.

Kokopelli: Casanova of the Cliff Dwellers, by John Young. Filter Press, Palmer Lake, Colorado, 1990.

Kokopelli: Flute Player Images in Rock Art, by Dennis Slifer and James Duffield. Ancient City Press, Santa Fe, New Mexico, 1994.

Life in the Pueblos, by Ruth Underhill. Ancient City Press, Santa Fe, New Mexico, 1991.

Stone Magic of the Ancients, by James R. Cunkle and Markus A. Jacquemain. Golden West Publishers, Phoenix, Arizona, 1995.

A.D. 1250: Ancient Peoples of the Southwest, by Lawrence W. Cheek. Arizona Highways Books, Phoenix, Arizona, 1994.

The People: Indians of the American Southwest, by Stephen Trimble. School of American Research Press, Santa Fe, New Mexico. 1993.

The Anasazi, by J. J. Brody. Rizzoli International Publications, Inc., New York, 1990

Watercarved stone bookends speak volumes. Courtesy of Arizona Highways

BUYER'S GUIDE

Again, our thanks to the following artists, galleries, and stores for providing the visuals for this book. Sources are listed alphabetically and include page numbers for the objects they refer to. A few items are not listed because the source is unknown or is no longer available. In some cases, both the manufacturer and retailer are listed.

47

Arizona Highways
The Arizona Center
455 North Third Street
Phoenix, AZ 85004
(602) 257-0381
bookends, page 46

Arizona Images
9622 East Metro Parkway,
Suite 1200
Phoenix, AZ 85051
(602) 861-2860
and
7014 East Camelback,
Suite 2100
Scottsdale, AZ 85251
(602) 990-1020
and
6555 East Southern,
Suite A-44
Mesa, AZ 85206
(602) 641-2941
Kokopelli's Kitchen products,
page 26

Arizona Sun Products
Scottsdale, AZ 85251
(602) 941-9067; (800) 442-4786
chip and dip bowl, page 37; clay
ornament, page 21 on the left

Blue Mountain Trading Post
P. O. Box 263
Blanding, UT 84511
(801) 678-2218
basket, page 1 and back cover

Coldwater Creek catalog
1 Coldwater Creek Drive
Sandpoint, ID 83864
(800) 968-0982
doormat, page xi

Esteban's at Tlaquepaque
P. O. Box 1462
Sedona, AZ 86339
(520) 282-4686
raku wall sculpture by Judy Kampa,
page 39

Fiesta Southwest Gifts
7121 East Fifth Avenue, #25
Scottsdale, AZ 85251
(602) 947-5699
sand globe ornament, page 21
on the right

Gina Designs
www.ginadesigns.com
Painted rusted metal wall
sculpture, page 42

Iron Craft
313 W. Sahuaro
Tucson, AZ 85705
(520) 740-0951
fireplace tools, page 36

Kactus Jock
7121 East Fifth Avenue
Scottsdale, AZ 85251
(602) 946-7566
Pelli-People, pages 16 and 17;
golf ball, page x; hat, page 52

Kennedy Indian Arts and Crafts
P. O. Box 6526
602 Montano Rd. NW
Albuquerque, NM 87107
(505) 344-7538
pottery, page 3

The Kitchen Source
112 E. Route 66
Flagstaff, AZ 86001
(520) 779-2302
towel, page viii

Kokopelli & Company
271 North Highway 89A
Sedona, AZ 86336
(520) 282-0529

Kokopelli's
2601 Washington
Midland, MI 48640
restaurant, page 29

Kokopelli Inn
6465 Highway 179
Sedona, AZ 86351
(888) SEE-KOKO
page 23

Kokopelli Records
P.O. Box 8200
Santa Fe, NM 87504
(505) 424-1250
compact disks, page 32

Kokopelli Winery
2060 North Haskell Avenue
Willcox, AZ 85643
(520) 384-3800
champagne, page 4; wine, page 24

Lazart Productions, Inc.
P.O. Box 1537
Gainesville, TX 76241
wall sculpture, page 42 on the right

Legart Illusions
1961 Main Street, #140
Watsonville, CA 95076
(800) 397-1777
www.legart.com
silk-screened stockings, page 4

Native Spirit
221 North Highway 89A
Sedona, AZ 86336
(520) 282-6282
money clip, page 25; wall
sculpture by Lazart Productions,
Inc., page 42 on the right; tiles,
pages 22 and 23

Nava Hopi Gallery
9608 North Metro Parkway
Phoenix, AZ 85051
(602) 678-5568
salt and pepper shakers, page 29;
napkins, page 29; snow globe,
page 15 and back cover

New West Galleries
211 North Highway 89A
Sedona, AZ 86336
(520) 282-9132
Kokopelli, wall sculpture by
Richard Forrest, cover and page iii;
Kokopelli, wall sculpture by Dutch
Walker, page 12 and back cover

Loona Otero Murals
P. O. Box 50232
Parks, AZ 86018
(520) 635-4259
mural, page 40

Qué Pasa
The Arizona Center
455 North Third Street
Phoenix, AZ 85004
(602) 253-6691
and
Fashion Square Mall
Scottsdale, AZ 85251
(602) 970-1987
copper ornament, page 21 in
the middle

Quintus, Inc.
P.O. Box 3930
Camp Verde, AZ 86322
(520) 567-3833
bookends, page 46

Rando's Indian Arts and Crafts
425 North Fourth Avenue
Tucson, AZ 85705
(520) 791-3355
button covers, page 18

Sculptured Arts
P. O. Box 20512
Sedona, AZ 86341
wall sculpture by Richard Forrest,
cover and page iii

Robert Shields Designs
P.O. Box 10777
Sedona, AZ 86339
(520) 204-2123
robertshields@sedona.net
www.robertshieldsdesign.com
silver necklace, page 20

Howard Sice, Artist
9901 East Stella Road
Tucson, AZ 85730
copper medallion on Central
Avenue in Phoenix, page 14

Don Stone, Stone Design
2110 E. Beaver Creek Rd.
McGuireville, AZ 86335
bookends, page 46

Table Talk
4823 North Twentieth Street
Phoenix, AZ 85016
(602) 381-6263
cookie cutters, page viii

TNT Smoke Shop
324 North Fourth Avenue
Tucson, AZ 85705
(520) 882-5584
box, page 18

Twin Rocks Trading Post
913 E. Navajo Twins Dr.
Bluff, UT 84512
(801) 672-2341; (800) 526-3448
basket, page 1

White Mountain
Archaeological Center
HC 30 Box 30
St. Johns, AZ 85936
(888) 333-5859
Kokopelli's Kitchen products,
page 26

Zonies Galleria
215 North Highway 89A
Sedona, AZ 86336
(520) 282-5995
Terra Cotta Clock *by Betty*
Timson, page ix; candle holder,
page 4; champagne glasses, page 4;
candy dish, page 6; Kokopelli
Stripe *cabinet, copyright © by Dan*
and Peg O'Leary, page 19; fire-
place set, page 36; raku wall sculp-
ture by Judy Kampa, page 39;
painted rusted metal wall sculpture
by Gina Designs, page 42

INDEX

*Page numbers in
italics refer to
photographs.*

50

Ad for kitchen-cabinet
company, ix
Air-brushed metal rendi-
tion, *cover, iii*
Amram, David, 25
Anasazi, 2, 4, 20, 35
accomplishments,
8–9
and farming, 6
imports from Central
America, 12
music, 9
pictographs, *ii, 7*
pottery, 9
settlements, 8
textiles, 9
Anderson, Ian, 16
Aphrodite, 38
Arizona Highways, 48
Arizona Images, 48
Arizona Sun Products,
48
Armstrong, Louis, 39
Art and crafts. *See also*
Jewelry, Knick-
knacks and
merchandise
air-brushed metal
rendition, *cover, iii*
candy vessel, *6*
gouache with foil on
paper, *vi*
hand-forged steel
with patina, *12,
back cover*
Hopi basket, 1, back
cover
kachina, *10*
mailbox stand, *45*
medallion on light
pole, *14,* 15
metal sculptures, *8,
12, 42, 44*
mural, *40*
painted ponderosa
pine, *19*
painted rusted metal,
42
petroglyphs, *xii,* 2,
11, *11,* 41–42
pictographs, *ii,* 2, *7*
sources, 48–50
watercarved stone
bookends, *46*

Author's encounters with
Kokopelli, ix–xi,
15, 37–43

Bacchus, 38–39
Basie, Count, 39
Beans, 6
Bed and breakfast
Kokopelli's Cave Bed
and Breakfast,
34–35
Beesinger, Jerry, 30
Beesinger, Louise, 30
Black, Bruce, 35
Blue Mountain Trading
Post, 48
Bookends, *46*
Buffett, Jimmy, 16
Burly Fish Tattoo and
Body Piercing, 19
Businesses named for
Kokopelli, 20, 25
Kokopelli, 33–34
Kokopelli Coffee and
Tea, 28
Kokopelli
Contemporary
Gallery, 30
Kokopelli Enterprises,
31–32
Kokopelli New Media
Development,
30–31
Kokopelli Products,
28–29
Kokopelli Records,
32–33, *32,* 49
Kokopelli's, 29
Kokopelli's Cave Bed
and Breakfast,
34–35
Kokopelli's Kitchen
Gourmet Specialty
Foods, 26–27, *26*
Kokopelli's Pizza
International, 33

Cafes and coffee shops,
25
Kokopelli Coffee and
Tea, 28
Canadian youth choir, 25
Candy vessel, *6*
Chaco Canyon, 8

Cigarette lighter, *x*
Clock, *ix*
Clothing store
Kokopelli, 33–34
Coldwater Creek catalog,
48
Cookies, *viii*
Corn, 6
Coyote, x, *42*
Cultural appropriation,
19–20
Cunkle, Carol, 26–27
Cunkle, James, 6, 20, 27

Darrow, Clarence, 43
Dawangyumptewa,
David, iv
Deer Valley Rock Art
Center, 21–22
Design firm
Kokopelli New Media
Development,
30–31
Dexter, Lanny, 29
Dome, *15, back cover*
Dragonflies, 13

Estebán, 8
Esteban's at
Tlaquepaque, 48

Fiesta Southwest gifts,
48
Fireplace tools, *36*
Flute, 3, 9–10, 41
Food products
Kokopelli's Kitchen
Gourmet Specialty
Foods, 26–27, *26*
Four Corners area, 2

Geisler, Jim, 32–33
Gift shop
Kokopelli
Contemporary
Gallery, 30
Gina Designs, 42, 48
Golf ball, *x*
Golf courses, ix, 25
Gonzalez, Victor, 22
Gouache with foil on
paper, *vi*

Hair salons, 25

Hand-forged steel with patina, *12, back cover*
Heard Museum, 20
Hohokam, 2, 4
Honyaktewa, James, 3
Hopi, 4, 9, 13, 18, 20
    basket, *1, back cover*
The Hunt, 8

Insects, 13
Iron Craft, 49
Ivins, Jim L., 42

Jethro Tull, 16
Jewelry, *18*
    belt buckle, *3*
    money clip, *25*
    "Rabbi-pelli" pendant, 20

Kachina
    in business names, 20
    Kokopelli, *10*
    religion, 2
Kactus Jock, 49
Katsina. *See* Kachina
Kelley, Riley, 31–32
Kennedy Indian Arts and Crafts, 49
Kenny G, 16, 23
The Kitchen Source, 49
Knickknacks and merchandise, ix–x
    candle holder, *4*
    ceramic tiles, 22
    cigarette lighter, *x*
    clock, *ix*
    dome, *15, back cover*
    figurines, 16–17
    fireplace tools, *36*
    golf ball, *x*
    night light, *x*
    place mats, 29, *29*
    in Sedona, 22
    serving plate, *37*
    sources, 48–50
    welcome mat, *xi*
Kokopelli
    author's encounters with, ix–xi, 15, 37–43
    in business names, 20, 25, 26–35
    characteristics of, 1–2, 45
    commercialization of

image, 20–22, 42
    contents of sack, 12–13
    current popularity and cultural significance, ix, xi, 1, 16, 18–20, 45
    difference between original and current figures, 2–3
    and farming culture, 6
    as fertility symbol, 5–6
    and flute, 3, 9–10, 41
    images in Sedona, 22
    and insects, 13
    interview with, 38–43
    kachina, *10*
    as man or god, 38–39
    "phallic ostentation," 4, 42
    and pop musicians, 13, 16–17, 23, 39
    as real person (Central American trader), 11–12
    roles of, 39–41
    and sex, 4, 5–6, 17–18
    symptoms of Pott's disease, 13
    and unexplained pregnancies, 5–6
    wild hair, 13, 41
    on World Wide Web, 25, 31, 35
Kokopelli (clothing stores), 33–34
Kokopelli Coffee and Tea, 28
Kokopelli Contemporary Gallery, 30
Kokopelli: Cultivation of Soul, 42
Kokopelli Enterprises, 31–32
Kokopelli Inn, 22, 23, 49
Kokopelli New Media Development, 30–31
Kokopelli Pods (self-storage lot), 25
Kokopelli Products, 28–29
Kokopelli Records, 32–33, 32, 49

Kokopelli Serenade, vi
Kokopelli Stripe, 19
Kokopelli Trail, 25
Kokopelli Winery, 25, 49
Kokopelli with Kolorfusion Finish, 42
Kokopellimana, 6–8
Kokopelli's, 29, 49
Kokopelli's Cave Bed and Breakfast, 34–35
Kokopelli's Kitchen Gourmet Specialty Foods, 26–27, 26
Kokopelli's Pizza International, 33

Lazart Productions, Inc., 49
Leg art, *4*
Legart Illusions, 49
Lincoln, Abe, 43
Lipka, Glen, 30–31
Locusts, 13
Lomahaftewa, Gloria, 20
Loona Otero Murals, 49

Mailbox stand, *45*
Maize, 6
Mann, Herbie, 33
Marley, Bob, 16, 39
Marley, Ziggy, 16
Marquis, Karen, 33–34
Medallion on light pole, *14, 15*
Mesa Verde National Monument and Park, 8, 34
Metal sculptures, *8, 12, 42, 44*
Mogollon, 2
Money clip, *25*
Morrison, Jim, 38
Mural, *40*

Native Americans and commercialization of Kokopelli, 20–21
Native Spirit, 49
Nava Hopi Gallery, 49
New West Galleries, 49
Night light, *x*

O'Leary, Dan, 19
O'Leary, Peg, 19
Otero, Loona, 40, 49

Painted rusted metal, *42*
Petroglyphs, *xii*, 2, 11,
    11, 41–42
Pevarnik, Steve, 8, 44
Phoenix, Arizona, ix, *14*,
    15, 20, 21, 45
Pictographs, *ii*, 2, 7
Pilles, Peter, 3–4
Pizza
    Kokopelli's Pizza
        International, 33
Pop musicians, 13,
    16–17, 23, 39
Pott's disease, 13
Pueblo Revolt of 1680, 8

Qué Pasa, 50
Quinn, Steve, 33
Quintus, Inc., 50

"Rabbi-pelli" pendant, *20*
Rando's Indian Arts and
    Crafts, 50
Raven Site Ruin, 26–27
Record company
    Kokopelli Records,
        32–33, *32*, 49
Restaurants, 25

Kokopelli's, 29
Kokopelli's Pizza
    International, 33
Richards, Keith, 16
Robber Flies, 13
Robert Shields Designs,
    50
Rock, Eleanor, iv, 1

Sculptured Arts, 50
Sedona, Arizona, 16
    images of Kokopelli,
        22
    Kokopelli Inn, 22, *23*,
        49
    Serving plate, *37*
Sex, 4, 5–6, 17–18
Sheehan, Rick, 28
Sice, Howard, 14, 50
Sinagua, 2
Smith, Mary, 33
Southwest, 2
Specialty foods, 26–27
Squash, 6
Street sign, *v*
Symphony, 25

Table Talk, 50

Taos Pueblo, 8
Tattoo, *19*
Taylor, Koko, 16
TNT Smoke Shop, 50
Twin Rocks Trading
    Post, 50

Walker, Dutch, iv, 12
Watercarved stone
    bookends, *46*
Welcome mat, *xi*
Welsh, Peter, 21–22
Werre, John, 28–29
White Mountain
    Archaeological
    Center, 26, 50
Wine bottle labels, *4, 24*
World Wide Web, 25, 31,
    35
Wright, Barton, 3, 18–19
Wupatki National
    Monument, *11*

Youvella, Tino, 10

Zonies Galleria, 50
Zuni, 4, 9, 20